I Use A Telescope

By Tracy Nelson Maurer

A Crabtree Seedlings Book

CRABTREE
Publishing Company
www.crabtreebooks.com

Table of Contents

I Use a Telescope

I use a telescope to see the Moon, stars, and planets in the night sky.

Sky Fact:
If you don't have a telescope, you can try using binoculars.

See The Moon?

See the Moon? Every night it rises in the east. It moves slowly across the sky. It sets in the west.

Does the Moon look like the letter "C"?
That's a **crescent moon**.

Does the Moon look like a ball?
That's a **full moon**. Moon **phases**
repeat about every four weeks.

crescent moon

full moon

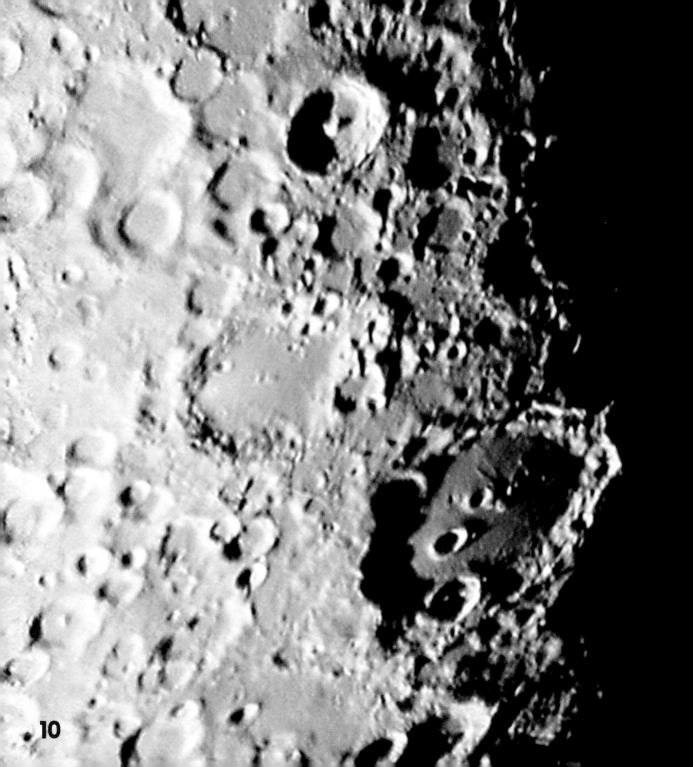

A telescope shows the Moon's **craters** and mountains.

See the Stars?

See the stars? Stars rise in the east and set in the west, just as the Moon does. Try to count them!

Sky Fact:
The Milky Way galaxy has 100 to 200 billion stars. The Sun is just one of them.

The Sun is a daytime star. At night, it shines on the other side of Earth.

Sky Fact:
The Sun is the closest star to Earth. It is about 93 million miles (150 million kilometers) away.

Star pictures are called **constellations.**

Look! The Big Dipper!

Sky Fact:
For centuries, travelers have used constellations to find their way.

The Big Dipper

See the Planets?

See the planets? Jupiter is the brightest and biggest planet near Earth.

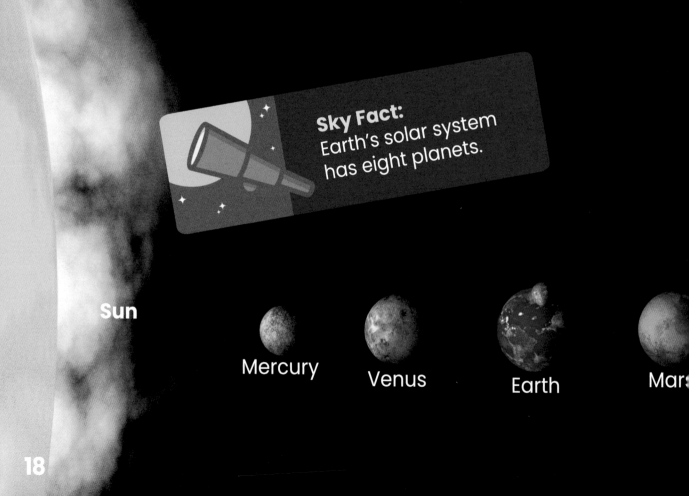

Sky Fact:
Earth's solar system has eight planets.

Sun

Mercury

Venus

Earth

Mars

Jupiter

Moon

Jupiter

Saturn

Uranus Neptune

19

Light Pollution

Light pollution hides the night sky.

I use my telescope away from the city.

What can YOU see in the night sky?

Glossary

constellations (kahn-stuh-LAY-shunz): Constellations are groups of stars that form a shape.

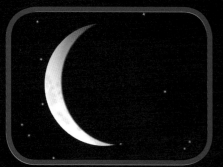

craters (KRAY-turz): Craters are large holes in the ground.

crescent moon (KRES-uhnt MOON): A crescent moon is the phase of the Moon when it looks thin and curved like the letter "C."

full moon (FUL MOON): A full moon is the phase of the Moon when it looks like a ball or circle.

light pollution (LITE puh-LOO-shun): Light pollution is too much light shining up from Earth.

phases (FAYZ-ez): Moon phases are the stages of the Moon's changing shape as it appears from Earth.

Index

School-to-Home Support for Caregivers and Teachers

This book helps children grow by letting them practice reading. Here are a few guiding questions to help the reader build his or her comprehension skills. Possible answers appear here in red.

Before Reading

- **What do I think this book is about?** I think this book is about how to use a telescope. I think this book is about what I can see with a telescope.

- **What do I want to learn about this topic?** I want to learn more about outer space. I want to learn about the stars in the sky and see them better.

During Reading

- **I wonder why...** I wonder why the Moon changes shapes. I wonder why the Sun is called a daytime star.

- **What have I learned so far?** I have learned that the Sun is the closest star to Earth. I have learned that Jupiter is the brightest and biggest planet near Earth.

After Reading

- **What details did I learn about this topic?** I have learned that star groups are called constellations. I have learned that for years travelers have used constellations to find their way.

- **Read the book again and look for the glossary words.** I see the word *craters* on page 11, and the word *constellations* on page 16. The other glossary words are found on pages 22 and 23.

Library and Archives Canada Cataloguing in Publication

Available at the Library and Archives Canada

Library of Congress Cataloging-in-Publication Data

Available at the Library of Congress

Crabtree Publishing Company

www.crabtreebooks.com   1–800–387–7650

Print book version produced jointly with Blue Door Education in 2023

Written by Tracy Nelson Maurer

Print coordinator: Katherine Berti

Printed in the U.S.A./072022/CG20220201

Content produced and published by Blue Door Education, Melbourne Beach FL USA. This title Copyright Blue Door Education. All rights reserved. No part of this book may be reproduced or utilized in any form or by any means, electronic or mechanical including photocopying, recording, or by any information storage and retrieval system without permission in writing from the publisher.

PHOTO CREDITS:
Cover and title page: Alohaflaminggo; telescope sky fact logo © plknyk; starry sky page header © Sergey Nivens: Page 2-3: shutterstock.com/ True Touch Lifestyle . page 4-5 © Alohaflaminggo; page 6-7 © Harold Stiver; page 9 © Andriy Lipkan; page 11 © Thomas Nord; page 12-13 © Anton Jankovoy; page 14-15 © Vladi333; page 16-17 © Allexxandar; page 18-19 © Computer Earth; page 20-21 © Sebastian Porral All images from Shutterstock.com except page 18 inset photo © Radoslaw Ziomber https://creativecommons.org/licenses/by-sa/4.0

Published in the United States
Crabtree Publishing
347 Fifth Ave.
Suite 1402-145
New York, NY 10016

Published in Canada
Crabtree Publishing
616 Welland Ave.
St. Catharines, Ontario
L2M 5V6